This book belongs to ____________________

Grand Canyon For Kids

JANE AND GARY FERGUSON
MIKE AND LITA EBERSOLE

Illustrated By
BONNIE JAKUBOS

Produced by GCBA Publishing
P.O. Box 292
Grand Canyon, Arizona 86023

printed on recycled paper

The earliest signs of humans in the Grand Canyon are small animal figures made from willow twigs. These objects, called "split-twig figurines", are 3000-4000

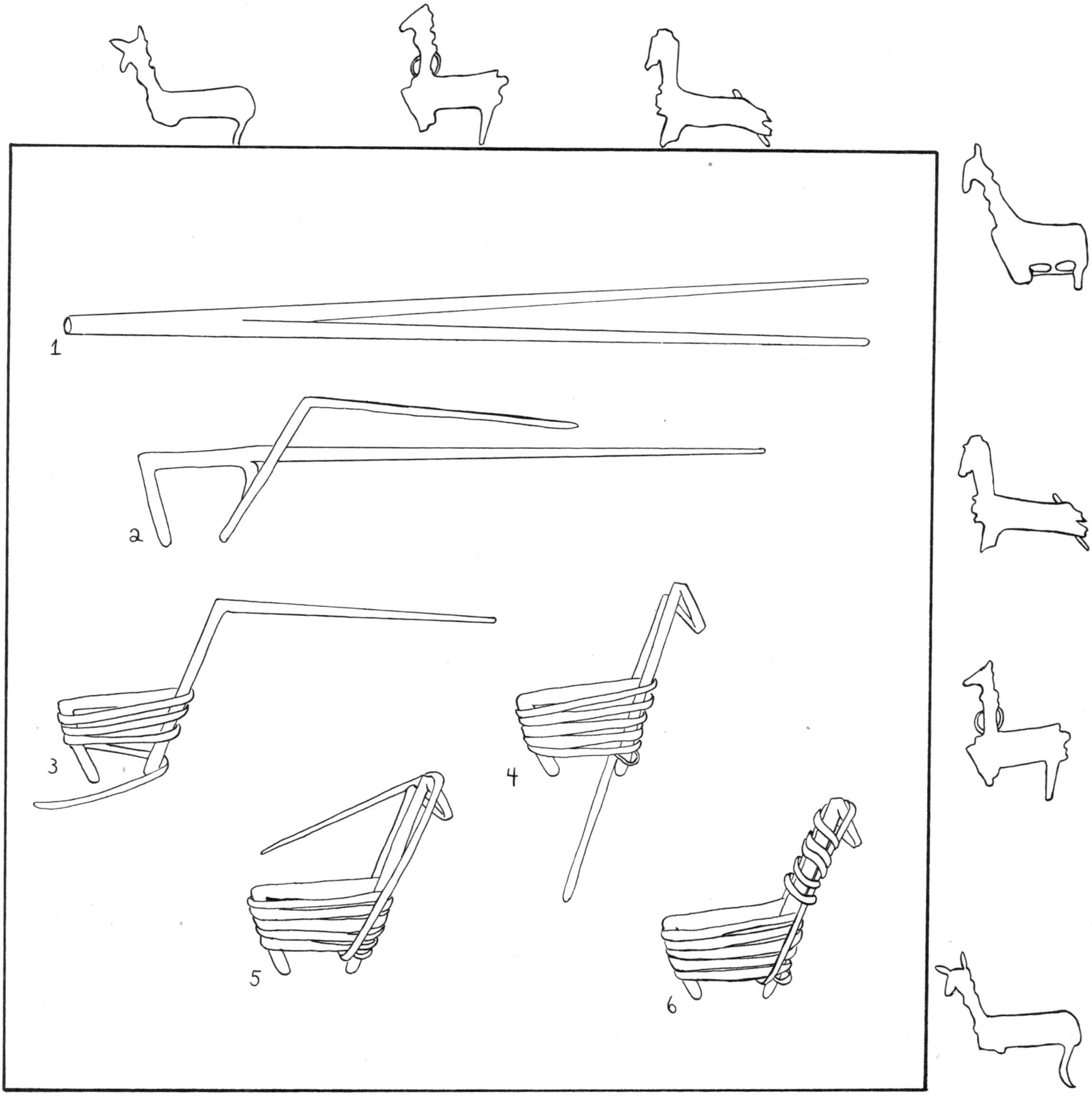

years old! We think that they were made by hunters from a group of people known as the Desert Culture. Use a thin strip of paper to make your own split-twig figurine.

Pictographs

My Pictograph

Another group of Indians lived in the Grand Canyon about 1,000 years ago. They are called Anasazi (An-ah-sah-zee). Anasazi is a Navajo (Nav-uh-hoe) Indian word which means "Ancient Ones." Anasazi drew pictures on the Canyon's rock walls of things or perhaps events that were special in their lives. These images are called pictographs. What might the creator of the above pictographs have been trying to say? Draw a pictograph of something about the Grand Canyon that is special to you.

Who Goes There?

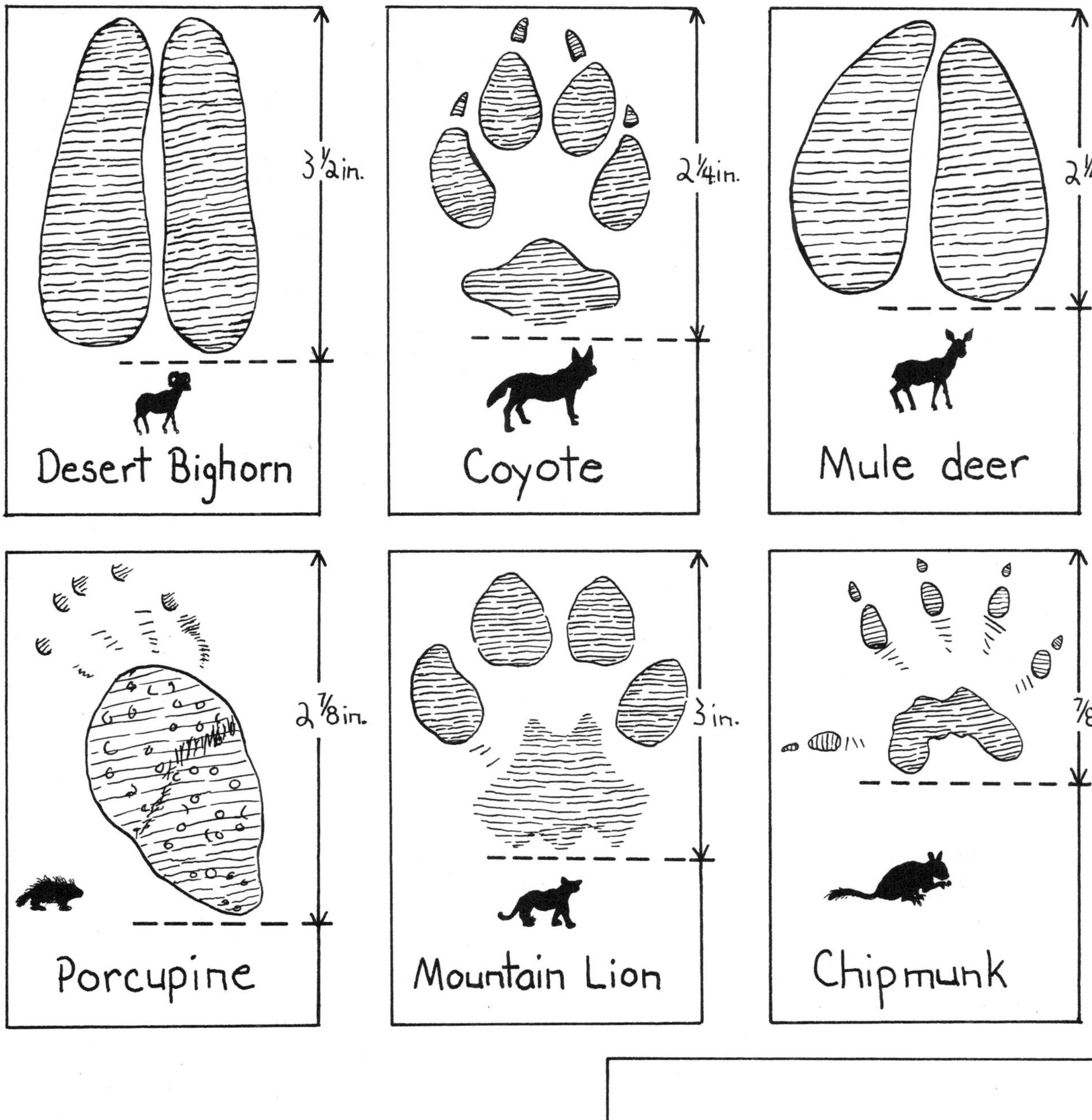

Can you find any other tracks? Draw them →

1=White

2=Gray

3=Brown

Before the Grand Canyon was here, this area had only one kind of tassel-eared squirrel. As the canyon formed, it split the animals into two groups. Living apart for thousands of years under different conditions has resulted in two kinds of squirrels, instead of one.

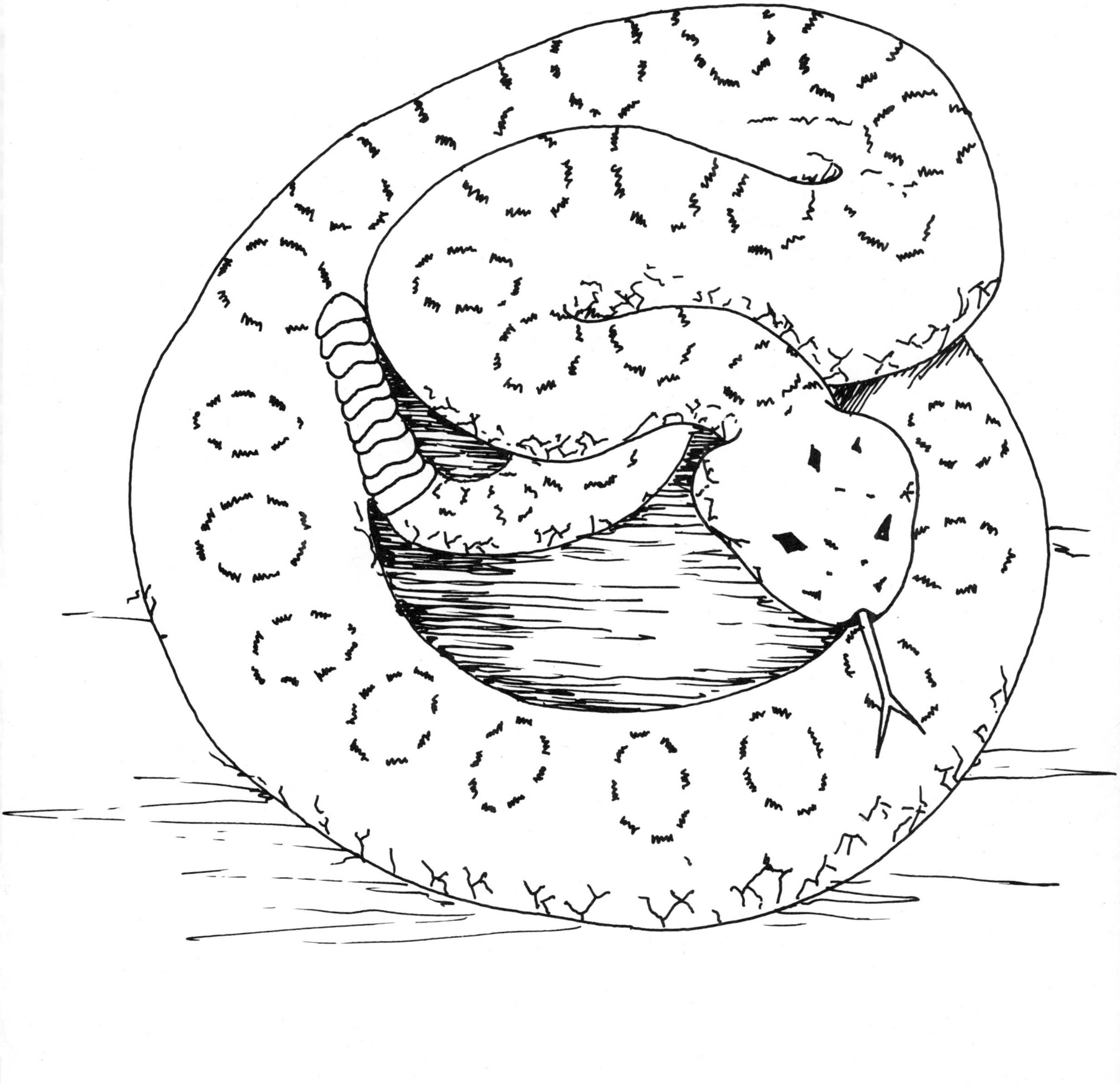

Here is the Grand Canyon rattlesnake. This is the only place in the world where it can be found. The snake's beautiful pink color helps it hide in the rocks of the canyon.

Color By Number

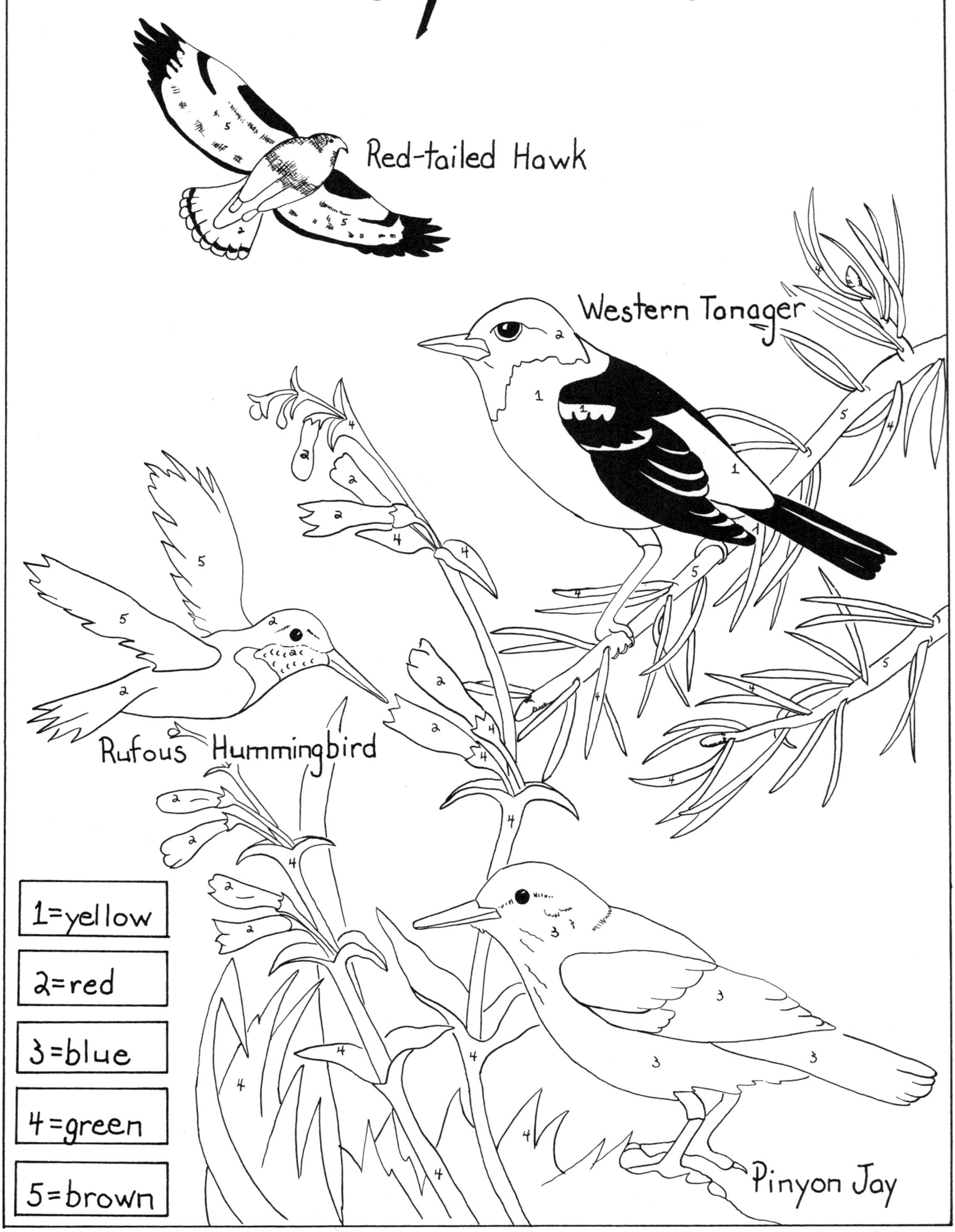

Tree Scramble

_ _ _ _ _ _ _ _

upecrs

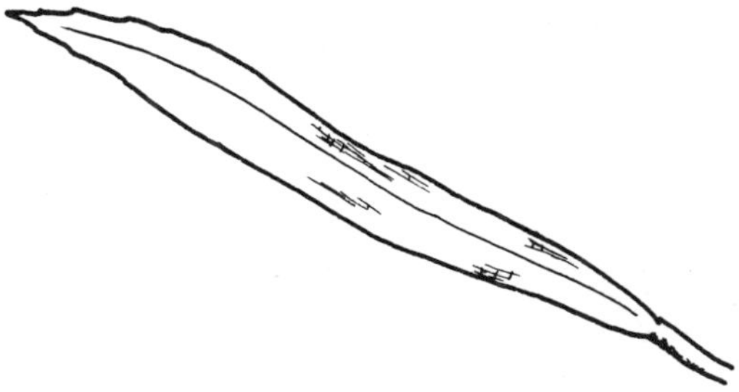

_ _ _ _ _ _ _ _ _ _ _ _

mabelG ako

_ _ _ _ _ _ _ _

illwow

_ _ _ _ _ _ _ _ _ _ _ _ _

aUht jirneup

_ _ _ _ _ _ _ _

ynoipn

_ _ _ _ _ _ _ _ _ _ _

nerosapod

Wildflower Fun

Paintbrush
(red-orange)

Yucca
(white)

Four O'clock
(purple)

W	G	Y	A	K	F	S	I	I
I	L	H	G	L	O	B	E	C
L	B	S	O	F	U	W	M	T
D	F	U	P	M	R	B	A	Y
F	Y	R	C	G	O	C	L	U
L	L	B	K	R	C	E	L	B
O	K	T	W	U	L	P	O	A
W	C	N	Y	A	O	C	W	N
E	I	I	F	R	C	C	T	M
R	R	A	E	P	K	Y	E	S
K	P	P	T	A	I	L	I	G

Gilia
(red)

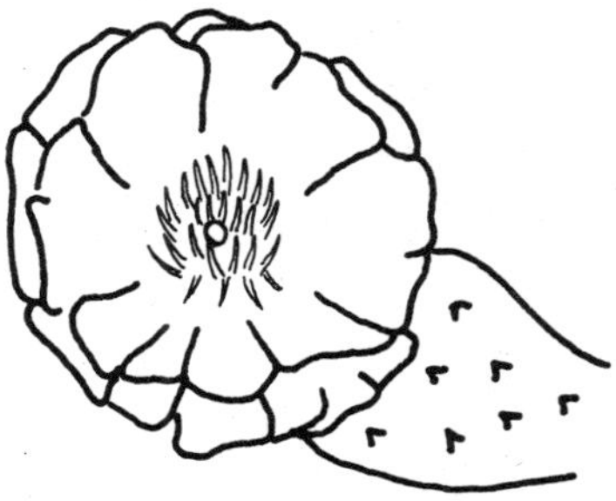

Prickly pear
(Pink)

Globe mallow
(orange)

All of these flowers are hidden in the above letters. Can you find and circle them? (Hint: they run up, down, across and diagonally. For flowers with two-part names, such as prickly pear, the words are not always together.) Can you find these flowers growing nearby?

Suppose you were a lizard living in the Grand Canyon. Where would you spend your days during the summer?

Why?

Imagine that you're on a raft trip down the Colorado River. Make a list of what you would take.

What if you were the Spanish explorer Don Lopez de Cardenas – the first European man to see the Grand Canyon more than 400 years ago? Write a letter to King Charles I of Spain, describing what you have seen.

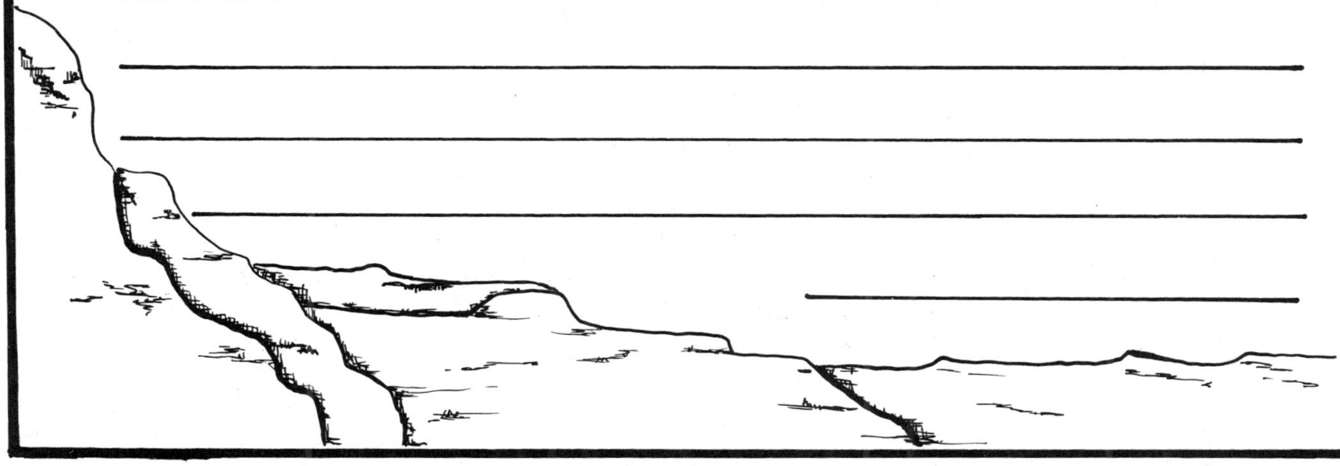

Down The Colorado

In 1869, John Wesley Powell and eight other men became the first to travel by boat through what is now Grand Canyon National Park. Relive their adventure!

1) Each player selects a marker (coins work great).

2) Order of play is according to age; youngest player moves first. For each turn, close your eyes and pick one crayon. Movement as follows:

   yellow - move forward one space
   green - move forward two spaces
   blue - lose one turn
   red - move back one space

3) First player to Grand Wash wins!

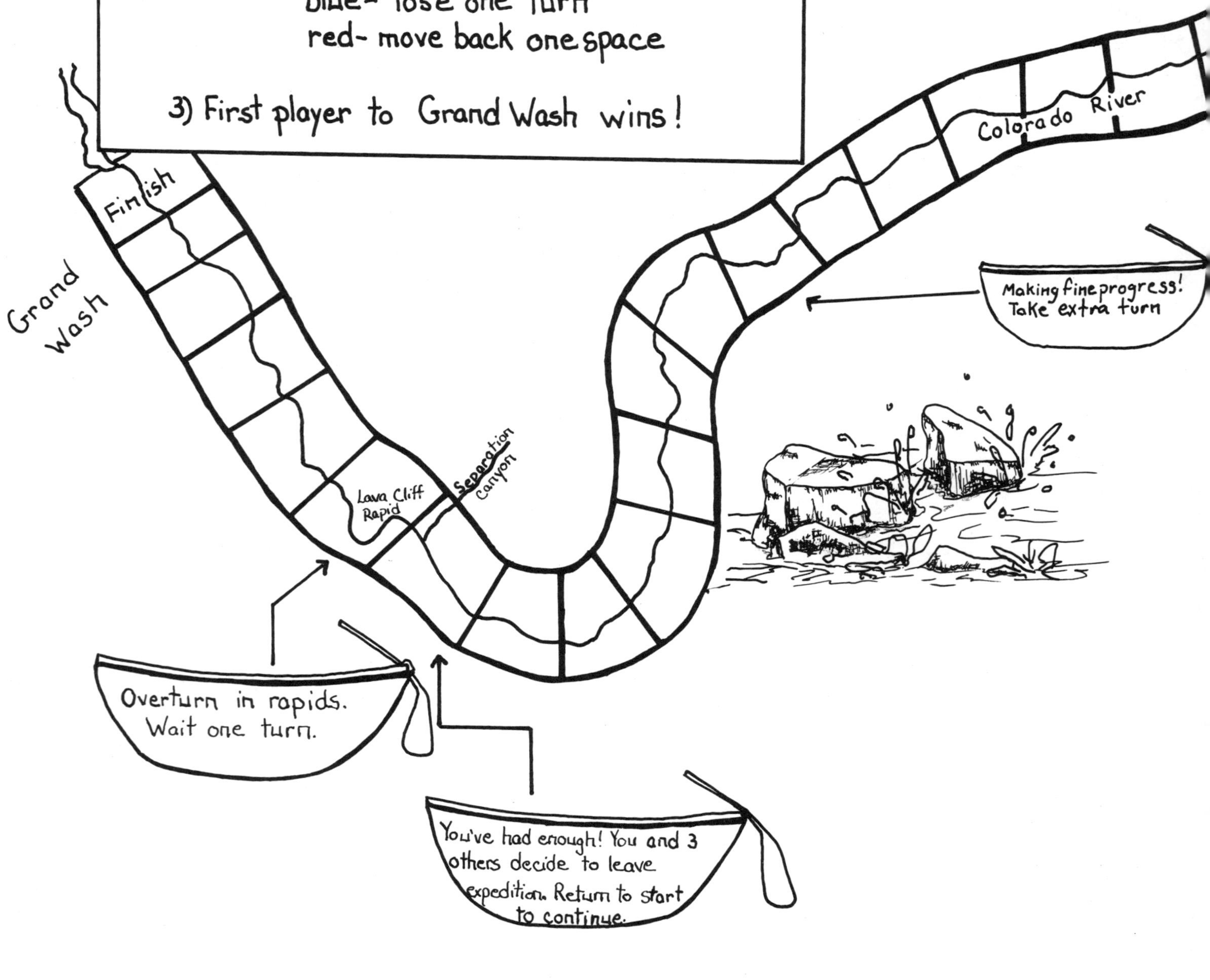

Start
Kanab Canyon
Havasu Canyon
Marble Canyon
Big rapids. Must line boots down river with ropes. Lose one turn.
Little Colorado River
Bright Angel Creek
Upper Granite Gorge
Food spoiling! Take extra turn to finish trip as quickly as possible.
Man overboard! Lose one turn.
Wait one turn to collect scientific specimens.
N

Barrel Cactus

Likes the hottest part of the Canyon.

Bighorn Sheep

Find him scrambling up the rocks between 3500 and 7000 ft.

Subalpine Fir

Can be found in the highest and wettest part of the park.

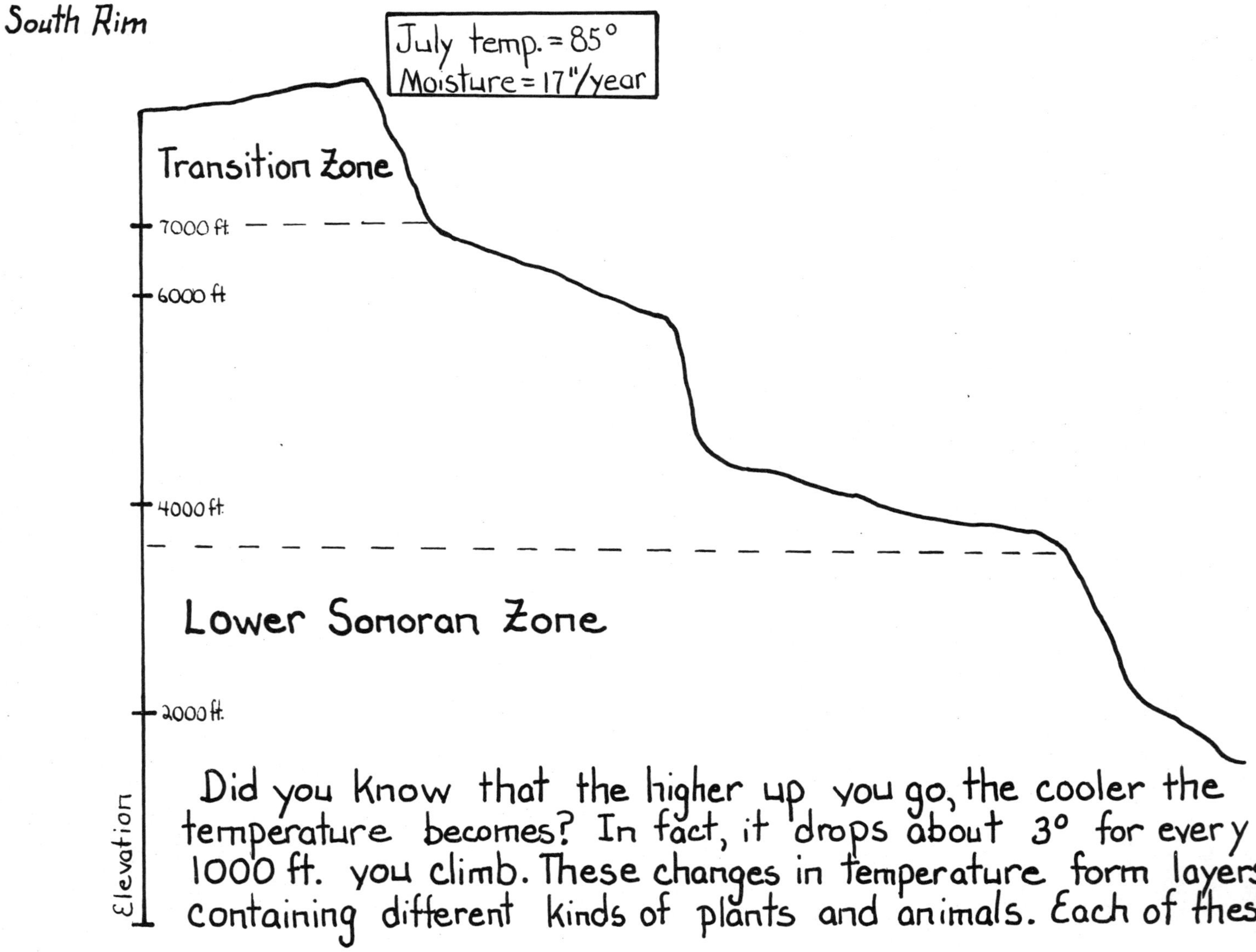

Did you know that the higher up you go, the cooler the temperature becomes? In fact, it drops about 3° for every 1000 ft. you climb. These changes in temperature form layers containing different kinds of plants and animals. Each of these

Whiptail Lizard

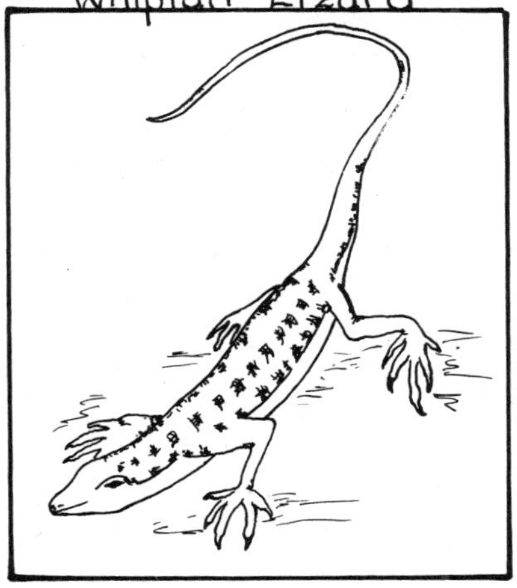

Lives in the part of the Canyon that receives the least amount of rainfall.

Raven

Can be seen flying along rock walls and ledges in the Upper Sonoran and Transition Zones.

Ponderosa Pine

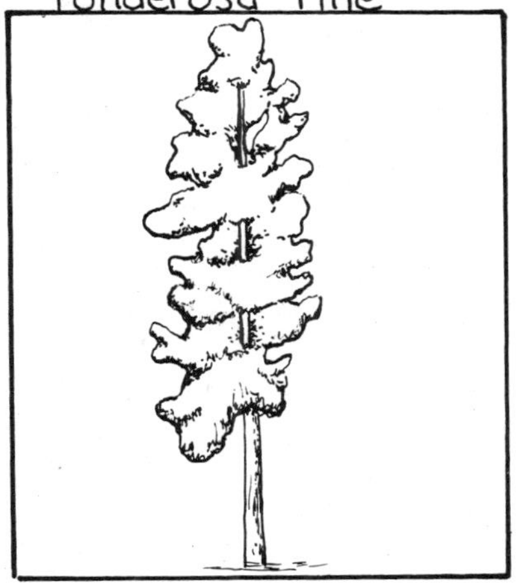

Seen in great numbers from 7000-8000 ft.

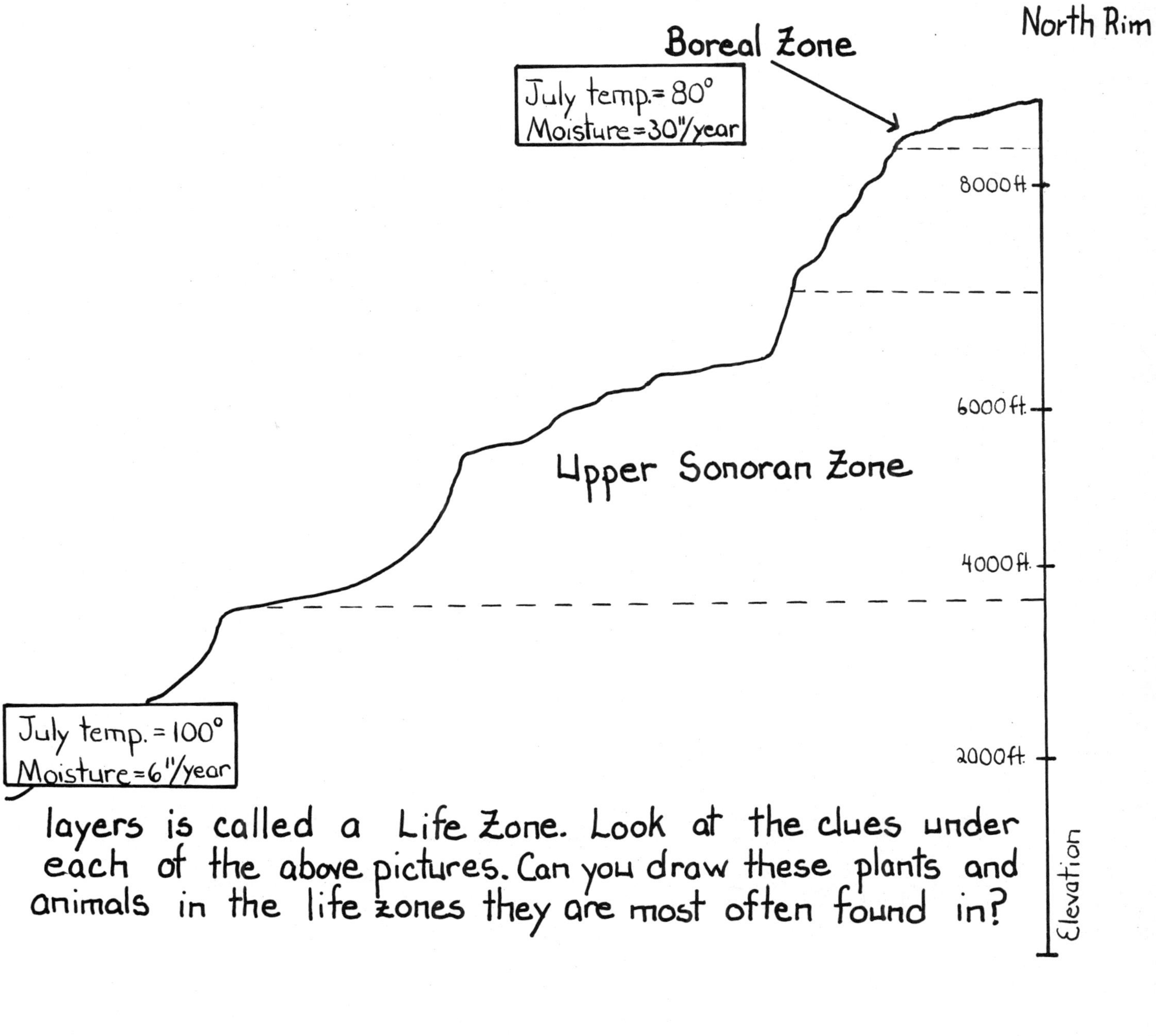

layers is called a Life Zone. Look at the clues under each of the above pictures. Can you draw these plants and animals in the life zones they are most often found in?

What's Wrong?

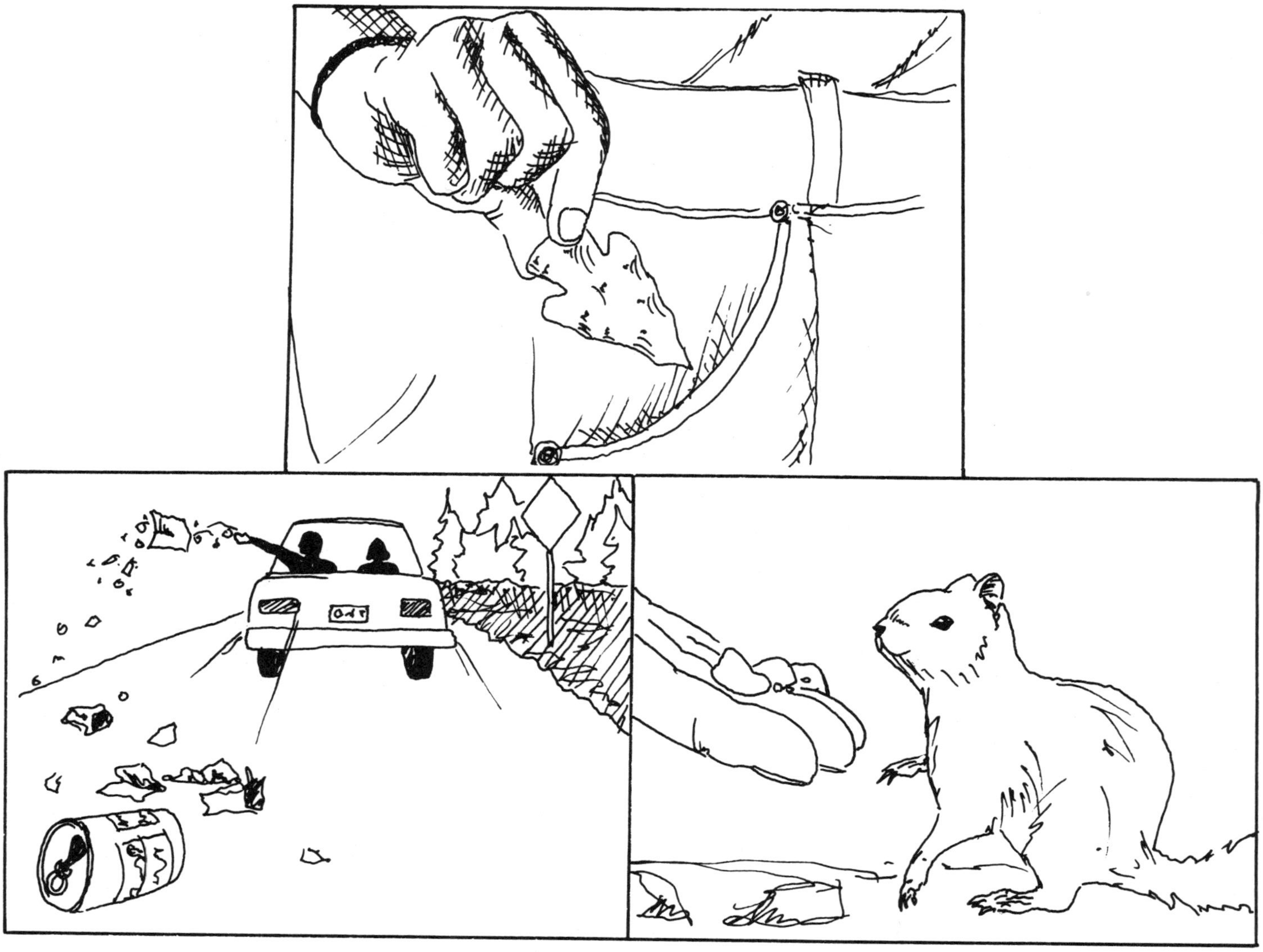

Each year, millions of people from all over the world visit the Grand Canyon. The Park needs your help if it is to remain such a special place. Explore the interesting things you find here, but then leave them for the next person to discover. Don't be a litterbug. And please, don't feed the animals.

Fossils

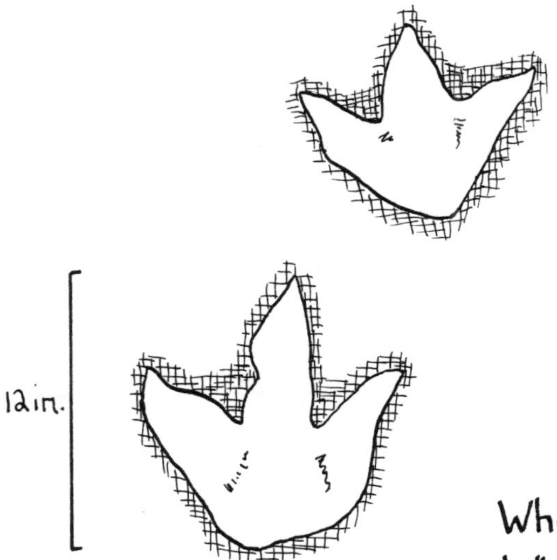

What? Dinosaur tracks
When? 150 million years ago
Where found? Painted Desert, east of Grand Canyon

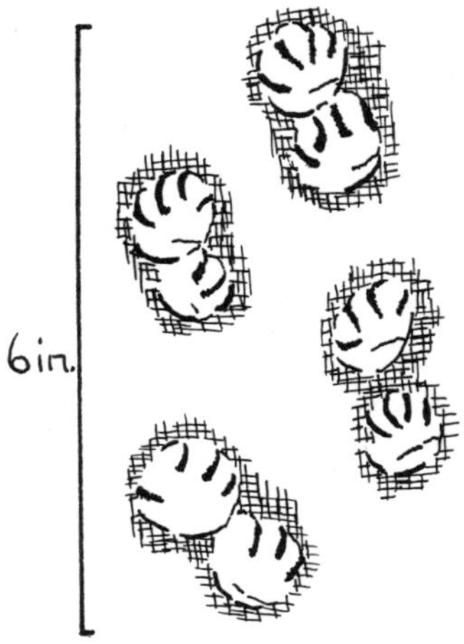

What? Reptile tracks
When? 270 million years ago
Where found? Along Hermit Trail, Grand Canyon

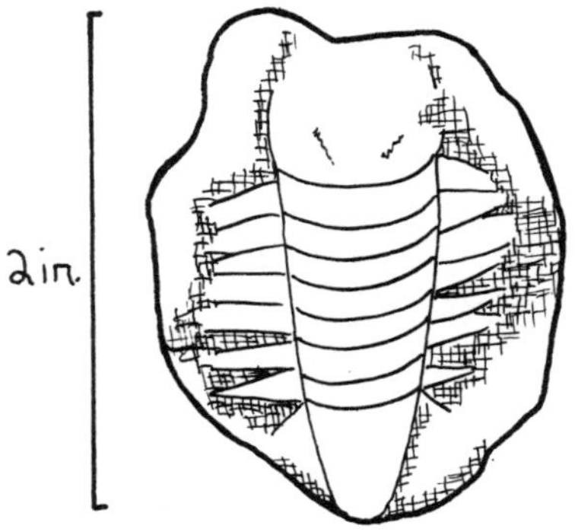

What? Trilobite
When? 500 million years ago
Where found? Near Indian Gardens, Grand Canyon

Fossils are the marks or remains of ancient plants and animals embedded in rock. There are many fossils in and around the Grand Canyon. What do you think the animals that left these fossils might have looked like? Draw a picture of each.

Two billion years ago the Grand Canyon looked like this- smoldering volcanos and thick beds of sediments and lava. Color these volcanos black!

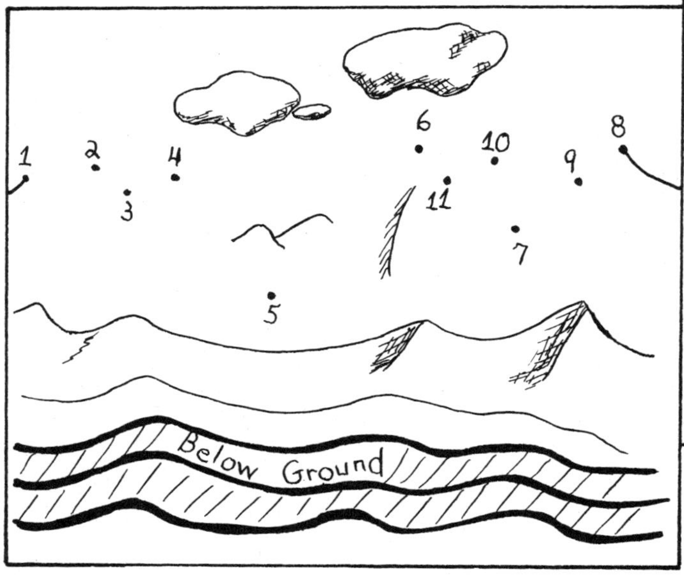

Over millions of years, pressures inside the earth pushed rock upward to form tall mountains. Connect the dots to see what the landscape looked like.

Then, inch by inch, water and wind wore away these mountains.

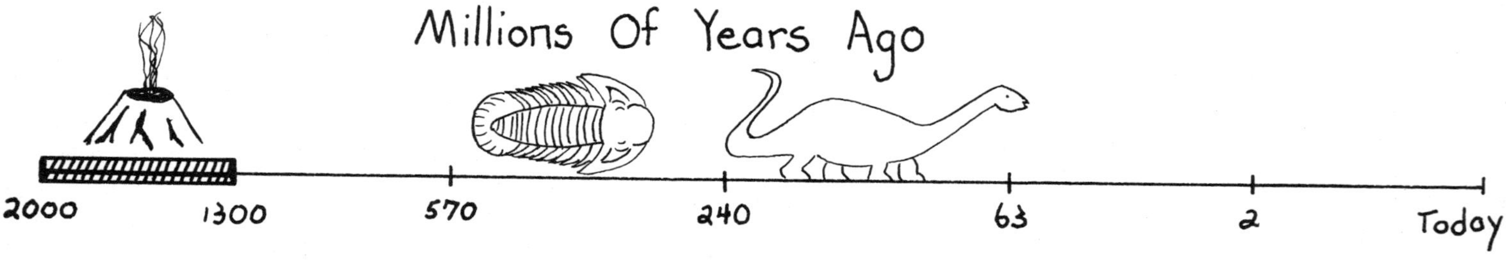

Movements in the earth's crust caused shallow oceans to invade this area. Over time, layers of mud and silt were laid down more than 2 miles thick!

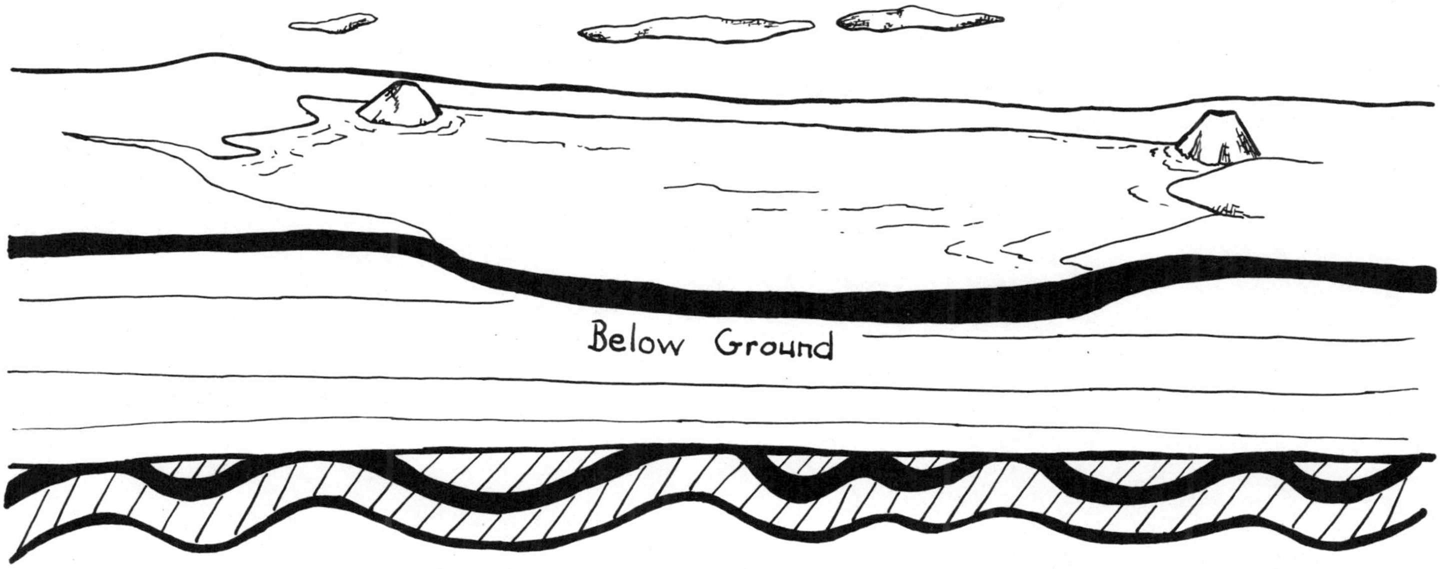

Connect the dots. Can you see how these mountains are different from those on the last page?

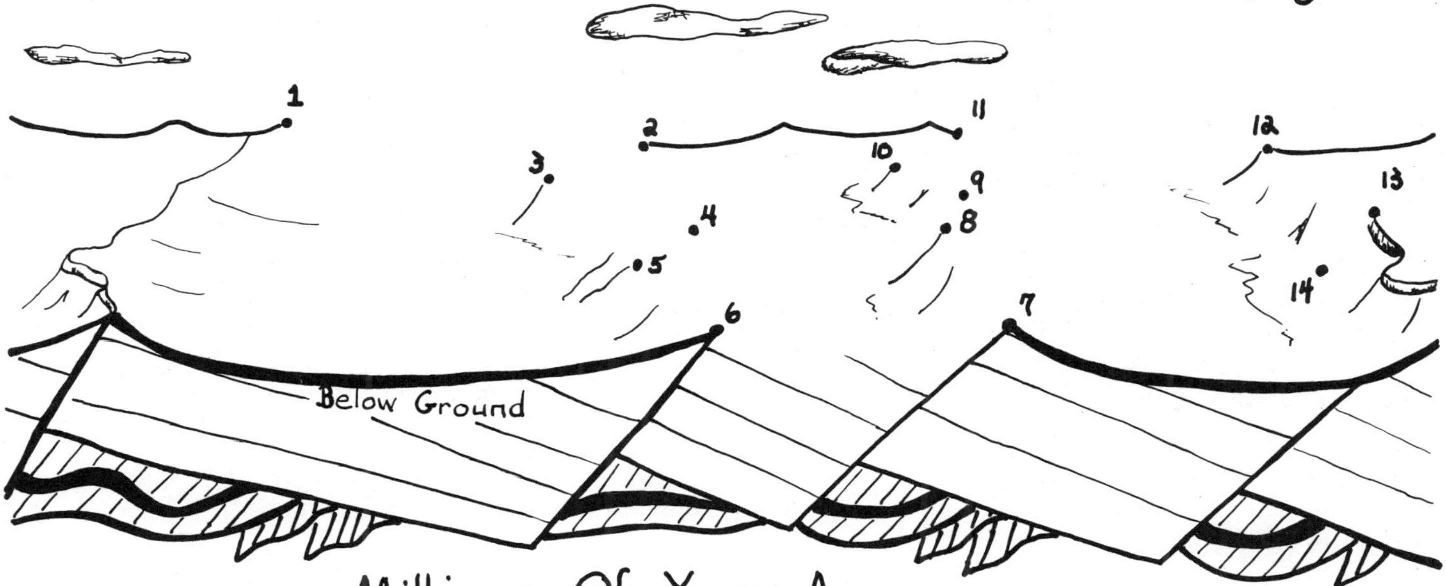

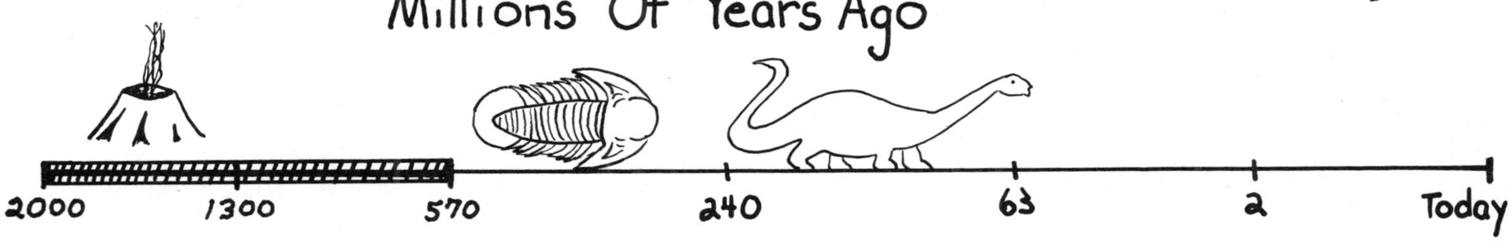

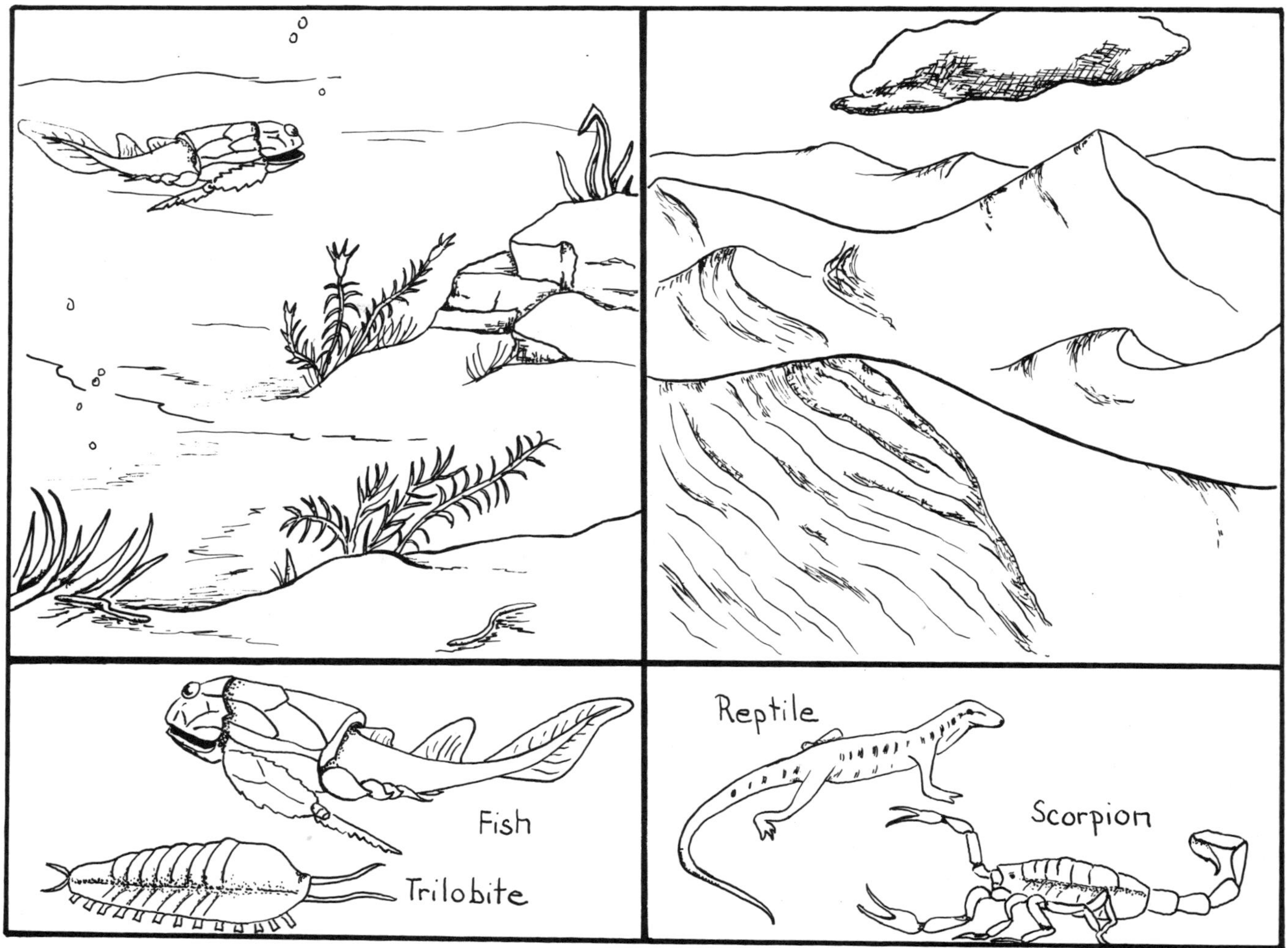

The next era of Grand Canyon history is known as Paleozoic (Pay-lee-o-zoh-ic). Paleozoic means "old life". During these 330 million years the land was covered with everything from shallow oceans to sand dunes. Above are some animals that lived during the Paleozoic era. Can you draw them in their homes?

Connect and Color

During the next 180 million years ocean sediments piled up over a mile thick. This era is called Mesozoic (Mess-so-zow-ic) and means "middle life". This was the age of dinosaurs. Traces of dinosaurs are sometimes found in rocks formed during this time. But at the Grand Canyon, most of these rocks have been worn away.

Millions of Years Ago

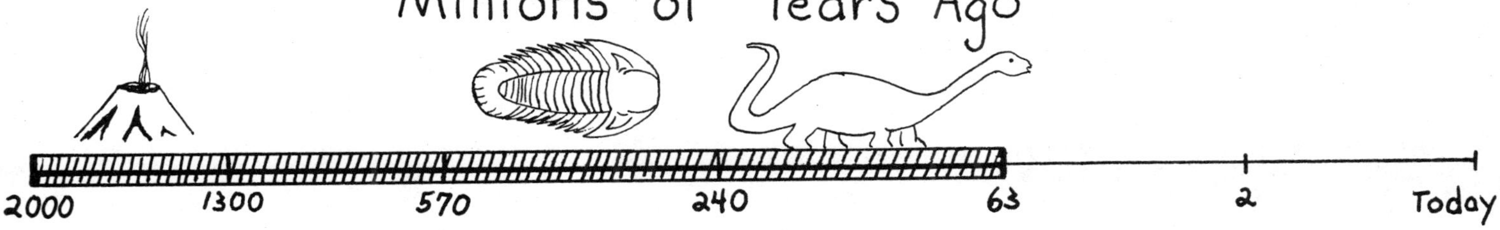

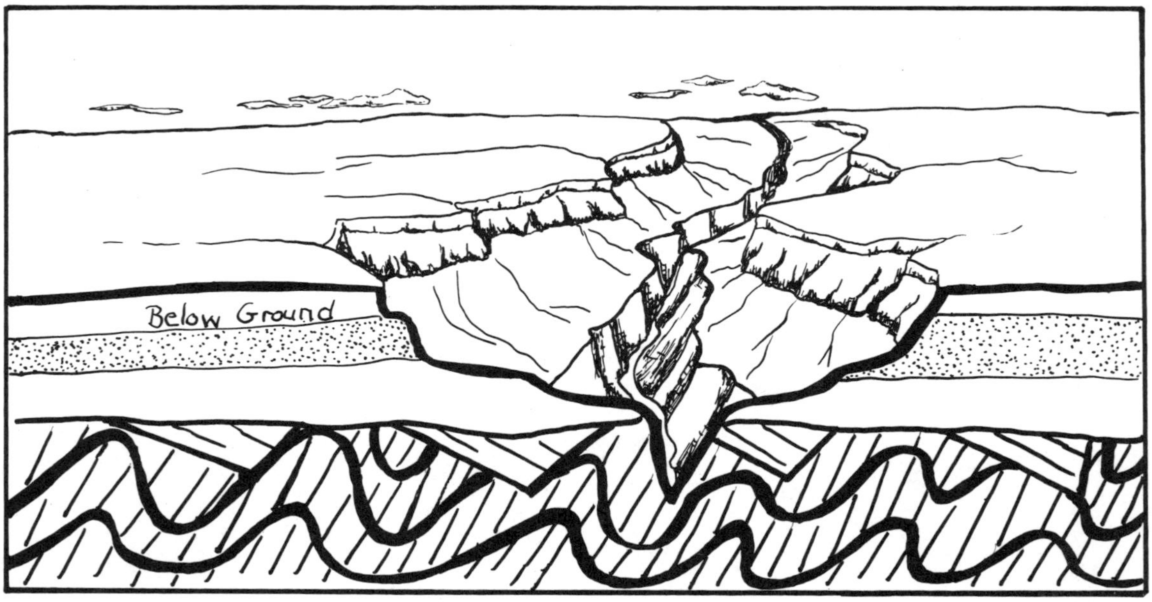

It has only been during the last few million years that the Colorado River has cut downward through the rock layers to form the Grand Canyon. This cutting action - along with the forces of wind, rain and ice - are changing the shape of these rocks even today. Draw a picture of how you think the canyon might look 3 million years from now.

Millions Of Years Ago

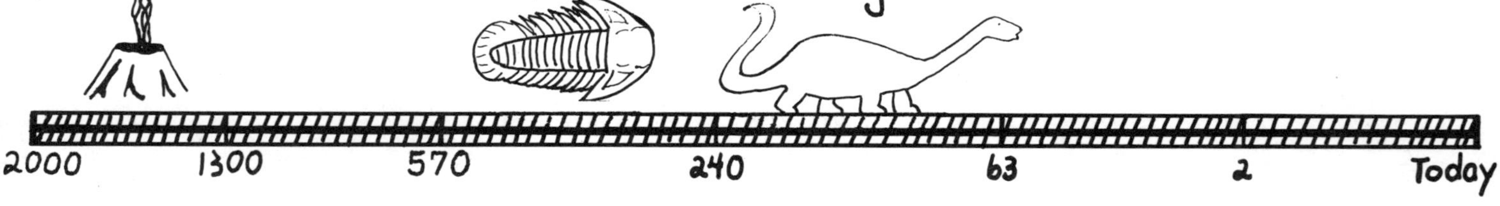

Each year, more than 350,000 people explore the backcountry of Grand Canyon National Park. (This is twice the number of people living in Las Vegas, Nevada!) Can you help these hikers find their way to Phantom Ranch? Please don't step on the plants and animals.

Did you Know that...

Great Horned Owl

1. every drop of water you use in this park has been pumped from a spring located on the north side of the river, several thousand feet below the Canyon rim?

2. the North Rim of the Grand Canyon is more than 1000 feet higher than the South Rim? Higher elevation means more moisture. In fact, during most winters over ten feet of snow falls on the North Rim.

3. before construction of an upriver dam, the Colorado River was cutting the Grand Canyon deeper at a rate of about 1 to 1½ inches each century?

4. near the Visitor Center the Canyon is ten times as wide as it is deep?

5. because Grand Canyon is a national park, it is being saved for your children and even your grandchildren to enjoy?

6. one out of every three people you see at the Grand Canyon is from a foreign country?

7. you can become a Junior Ranger? Go to the Visitor Center information desk to find out how!

8. Grand Canyon stretches more than 270 miles without a single road crossing?